the ZANIEST RIDDLE BOOK in the WORLD

by **JOSEPH ROSENBLOOM**
ILLUSTRATED by **SANDY HOFFMAN**

Sterling Publishing Co., Inc. **New York**

To Reba and Al Backerman

Library of Congress Cataloging in Publication Data

Rosenbloom, Joseph.
  Zaniest riddle book in the world.

  1. Riddles, Juvenile.   I. Hoffman, Sanford.   II. Title.
PN6371.5.R62   1984   818'.5402   83-18102
ISBN 0-8069-4680-6
ISBN 0-8069-4681-4 (lib. bdg.)

ISBN 0-8069-6252-6 (pbk.)

Copyright © 1984 by Joseph Rosenbloom
Published by Sterling Publishing Co., Inc.
387 Park Avenue South, New York, N.Y. 10016
Distributed in Canada by Sterling Publishing
% Canadian Manda Group, P.O. Box 920, Station U
Toronto, Ontario, Canada M8Z 5P9
Distributed in Great Britain and Europe by Cassell PLC
Artillery House, Artillery Row, London SW1P 1RT, England
Distributed in Australia by Capricorn Ltd.
P.O. Box 665, Lane Cove, NSW 2066
Manufactured in the United States of America

Contents

1. Animal Crack-Ups	5
2. Clothes-tro-phobia	14
3. Bad Guys	19
4. Fun & Games	23
5. E-I-E-I-Oh!	35
6. All Wet	41
7. Going Bananas	46
8. So What?	53
9. World Records	59
10. Home Sweet Home	63
11. Oops!	68
12. Love & Kisses	73
13. Greetings!	78
14. What's Your Line?	81
15. Peculiar Pets	86
16. School Daze	92
17. Sick & Tired	100
18. Sports Can Be Funny	106
19. Going Crazy	113
20. Monstermania	117
Index	125

Books by Joseph Rosenbloom

Bananas Don't Grow on Trees
Biggest Riddle Book in the World
Daffy Definitions
Doctor Knock-Knock's Official Knock-Knock
   Dictionary
Funny Insults & Snappy Put-Downs
Gigantic Joke Book
How Do You Make an Elephant Laugh?
Looniest Limerick Book in the World
Mad Scientist
Monster Madness
Official Wild West Joke Book
Polar Bears Like It Hot
Ridiculous Nicholas Haunted House Riddles
Ridiculous Nicholas Pet Riddles
Ridiculous Nicholas Riddle Book
Silly Verse (and Even Worse)
Wacky Insults and Terrible Jokes

1. Animal Crack-Ups

What does an aardvark like on its pizza?
Ant-chovies.

What is black and white and blue all over?
A zebra at the North Pole.

What is black and white and hides in caves?
A zebra who owes money.

What is black and white and has sixteen wheels?
A zebra on roller skates.

A zebra with wide stripes married a zebra with narrow stripes. Their first son had no stripes. What did they call him?
Arthur.

How are people like animals?
We have bare (bear) feet, frogs in our throats, calves on our legs and bull on our tongues.

Can giraffes have babies?
No, they can only have giraffes.

Why are giraffes so slow to apologize?
It takes a long time for them to swallow their pride.

Does a giraffe get a sore throat if it gets wet feet?
Yes, but not until the following week.

What would you get if you crossed a giraffe with a rooster?
You'd get an animal that wakes people who live on the top floor.

What is gray on the inside and clear on the outside?
An elephant in a Baggie.

What is gray and blue and very big?
An elephant holding its breath.

What is yellow, then gray, then yellow, then gray?
An elephant rolling downhill with a daisy in its mouth.

How can you tell if an elephant is visiting your house?
His tricycle will be parked outside.

What do you get if you cross an elephant and a canary?
A messy cage.

How do elephants speak to each other?
On 'elephones.

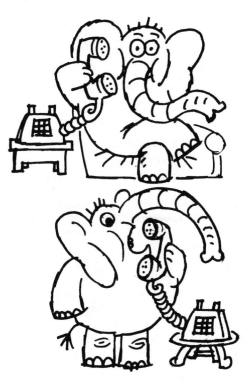

What is black and white, black and white, black and white and green?
Three skunks eating a pickle.

What does a skunk do when it gets angry?
It raises a stink.

What would you get if you crossed a skunk and a banana?
I don't know what you'd call it, but it would have a yellow stripe down the middle.

How can you tell an elephant from spaghetti?
The elephant doesn't slip off the end of your fork.

What do you get if you cross an elephant and a jar of peanut butter?
You get a peanut butter sandwich that never forgets.

Is it hard to spot a leopard?
No, they come that way.

8

How many different kinds of gnus are there?
Two. Good gnus and bad gnus.

How do rabbits travel?
By hareplane.

Do rabbits use combs?
No, they use hare brushes.

What would you get if 120 rabbits took one step backwards at the same time?
A receding hair line.

What would you get if you crossed a rabbit and a lawn sprinkler?
Hare spray.

What would you get if you blew your hair dryer down a rabbit hole?
Hot cross bunnies.

How do you make a poisonous snake cry?
Take away its rattle.

What weighs 5,000 pounds, eats peanuts and lives in Los Angeles?
An L.A. Phant.

Why are elephants so smart?
Because they have lots of gray matter.

What is brown, has a hump, and lives at the North Pole?
A lost camel.

9

How can you tell which end of a worm is its head?

Tickle it in the middle and see which end laughs.

What is yellow and sucks sap from trees?

A yellow-bellied sap sucker.

How do you keep an elephant from going through the eye of a needle?

Tie a knot in its tail.

Why do elephants have short tails?

So they won't get stuck in revolving doors.

If there are four sheep, two dogs and one herdsman, how many feet are there?

Only two. Sheep have hooves; dogs have paws; only people have feet.

What do you get if you cross a sheep and a porcupine?

An animal that knits its own sweaters.

What do you get if you cross a skunk and a raccoon?

A dirty look from the raccoon.

What do you get if you cross a skunk and a gorilla?

I don't know what you'd call it, but it wouldn't have any trouble getting a seat on the bus.

What do you call a 2,000-pound gorilla?
"Sir."

What is the best thing to do if you find a gorilla in your bed?
Sleep somewhere else.

What kind of tool do you use to fix a broken gorilla?
A monkey wrench.

What language do chimpanzees speak?
Chimpanese.

How do you take down a monkey's voice?
With an ape recorder.

What kind of apes grow on vines?
Gray apes (grapes).

What animal has eyes that cannot see, legs that cannot move, but can jump as high as the Empire State Building?
A wooden horse. The Empire State Building can't jump.

When is a horse not a horse?
When it turns into a pasture.

Why is it hard to recognize horses from the back?
Because they're always switching their tails.

A donkey was tied to a rope six feet long. A bale of hay was 18 feet away and the donkey wanted to eat the hay. How could he do it?
Easily. The rope wasn't tied to anything.

What use is a reindeer?
It makes the flowers grow, sweetie.

What has antlers and eats cheese?
Mickey Moose.

How can you tell a boy moose from a girl moose?
By his moustache.

What animal do you look like when you're in the shower?
A little bear.

How do you get fur from a bear?
By car, bus, train or plane.

What do you get if you cross a hyena and a parrot?

> *An animal that laughs at its own jokes.*

What happens if you cross a lion and a goat?

> *You have to get a new goat.*

Why did the turtle cross the road?

> *To get to the Shell station.*

Why did the otter cross the road?

> *To get to the otter side.*

Why did the elephant cross the road?

> *It was the chicken's day off.*

How is a chicken stronger than an elephant?

> *An elephant can get chicken pox, but a chicken can't get elephant pox.*

Why does an elephant want to be alone?

> *Because two's a crowd.*

What do you call pigs who write letters to each other?

> *Pen pals.*

How mad can a kangaroo get?

> *Hopping mad!*

2. Clothes-tro-phobia

What did the comedian say when he took off his clothes?
"Haven't you ever seen a comic strip?

What clothing does a house wear?
Address.

What is the difference between a dressmaker and a nurse?
One cuts dresses, the other dresses cuts.

How are cities dressed?
With outskirts.

How can you get four suits for a dollar?
Buy a deck of cards.

When is a man like a suit of clothes?
When his tongue has a coat and his breath comes in short pants.

What likes to spend the summer in a fur coat and the winter in a wool bathing suit?
A moth.

What do you get if you cross a moth and a firefly?
An insect that finds its way around dark closets.

What do you get if you cross a telephone and a shirt?
Ring around the collar.

What kind of suit does a duck wear?
A duck-sedo (tuxedo).

What do rich turtles wear?
People-necked sweaters.

What are a dog's clothes made of?
  Mutt-terial.

Where do frogs hang up their coats?
  In the croak room.

What kind of shoes do frogs like?
  Open toad shoes.

What is six feet long, green and has two tongues?
  The Jolly Green Giant's sneakers.

What shoes should you wear when your basement
is flooded?
  Pumps.

When a tailor presses your pants, is it all right to scream?

Yes, if you're still in them.

What are Van Winkle trousers?

Pants with a Rip in them.

What did one side of the pants say to the other side of the pants?

"Let's split!"

What kind of ties can't you wear?

Railroad ties.

What always speaks the truth but doesn't say a word?

A mirror.

What did the mirror say to the dresser?

"I see your drawers."

A man opened a piece of furniture and a dozen people fell out. Why?

Because it was a missing persons bureau.

What is beautiful, gray and wears glass slippers?

Cinderelephant.

If you saw nine elephants walking down the street with red socks and one elephant walking down the street with green socks, what would this prove?

That nine out of ten elephants wear red socks.

What did the sock say to the foot?
  "You're putting me on."

What did one stocking say to the other stocking?
  "So long now, I gotta run."

What do you get when you tear a scarf in two?
  A bandana split.

3. Bad Guys

Did you hear about the outlaws who went sky diving?
They had a chute out.

What was the name of the most famous pickle gangster?
Dill-inger.

What did the razor blade say to the razor?
"Schick 'em up!"

What did the victim say when the robber stuffed his mouth with a dirty cloth?
"That's an old gag."

What kind of bars can't keep prisoners in jail?
Chocolate bars.

Why did the burglar take a bath before breaking out of jail?
To make a clean getaway.

How is an escaping prisoner like an airplane pilot?
They both want safe flights.

What happened when the police caught the frank-furter?

They grilled it.

What is the difference between the law and an ice cube?

One is justice and the other is just ice.

Why are potatoes good detectives?

Because they keep their eyes peeled.

What two garden vegetables fight crime?

Beetman and Radish.

What kind of person steals soap?

A dirty crook.

Why was the belt arrested?

For holding up the pants.

What happens to people who steal watches?

The lawyer gets the case and the judge gives them time.

How did the intruder get into the house?

Intruder (in through the) door.

What happens to a thief if he falls into a cement mixer?

He becomes a hardened criminal.

What did the criminal say when he was saved from the hangman at the last minute?

"No noose is good noose."

How is a freezing elephant like a spy?
Both have a code in their trunks.

What kind of eyeglasses do spies wear?
Spy-focals.

Why did the spy spray his room with DDT?
He thought it was bugged.

Why don't they ever make counterfeit pennies?
That would be non-cents (nonsense).

What were the picture's last words?
"First they frame me, then they hang me."

What do you call stolen candy?
Hot chocolate.

What would you get if you crossed a rodent with a machine gun?
I don't know what you'd call it, but it would go "rat-a-tat-tat."

4. Fun & Games

What is a big frog's favorite game?
Croquet.

What is a little frog's favorite game?
Hop Scotch.

What is a mouse's favorite game?
Hide-and-Squeak.

What was Dr. Jekyll's favorite game?
Hyde and Seek.

What game do baby chickens play?
Peck-a-boo.

What television game is most popular with fishes?
"Name that Tuna."

What kind of television program do you see in the morning?
A breakfast serial (cereal).

What is a comedian's favorite breakfast cereal?
Cream of wit.

What is the difference between a comedian and a gossip?

A comedian has a sense of humor; a gossip has a sense of rumor.

What is the difference between a mirror and a gossip?

One reflects without speaking; the other speaks without reflecting.

What do you call a funny book about eggs?

A yolk book.

What do you get when you saw a comedian in two?

A half wit.

How do you make a pickle laugh?
Tell it an elephant joke.

How does a quiet Hawaiian laugh?
With a low ha (aloha).

What do you get if you cross a Hawaiian dancer and an Indian brave?
A hula-whoop.

When do comedians take milk and sugar?
At tea-hee time.

What kind of tea do the king and queen drink?
Royalty.

Why shouldn't you play with matches?
Because you could make an ash of yourself.

When is it dangerous to play cards?
When the joker is wild.

Why couldn't Noah play cards on the ark?
The elephant was standing on the deck.

What kind of illumination did Noah use on the ark?
Floodlights.

What phrase is heard most often at pickle card games?
"Dill me in."

When should you put a band-aid on a pack of playing cards?

When someone cuts the deck.

Which member of the ship's crew puts away the playing cards?

The deck hand.

What kinds of toys does a psychiatrist's child play with?

Mental blocks.

What do you get if you cross a small horn and a little flute?

A tootie flooty.

What do you get if you cross a hyena and a collie?

An animal that laughs through Lassie movies.

What makes a chess player happy?

Taking a knight off.

What is the difference between a ball and a prince?

One is thrown to the air; the other is heir to the throne.

What kind of ball is fun to play with but doesn't bounce?

A snowball.

Where do fortune tellers dance?

At the crystal ball.

Why are four-legged animals such poor dancers?
You would be, too, if you had two left feet.

What do dancers get when they eat too much?
Ballet-aches (belly-aches).

What punctuation mark is used in writing dance music?
The polka dot.

What do you call a lion tamer who puts his right arm down a hungry lion's throat?
   Lefty.

Who is safe when a man-eating lion is loose?
   Women and children.

What is the last thing a trapeze flyer wants to be?
   The fall guy.

Can you figure out this metric puzzle? If you are blindfolded and move one meter to the right, and then three-quarters of a meter to the left, and then go west for one-half a meter, where will you be?
   In the dark. (Remember, you were blindfolded.)

28

What do frogs drink at snacktime?
  Croak-a-Cola.

What does the Invisible Man drink at snacktime?
  Evaporated milk.

Why shouldn't you cry over spilled milk?
  It gets too salty.

What kind of soda can't you drink?
  Baking soda.

Why are stupid people like decaffeinated coffee?
  Because there is no active ingredient in the bean.

What is a tree's favorite drink?
  Root beer.

What happened to the boy who drank eight Cokes?

He burped 7-up.

Who is the thirstiest person in the world?

The one who drank Canada Dry.

What instrument does a lighthouse keeper play?

The fog horn.

What do you get if you cross a banana and a comedian?

Peels of laughter.

What do you get if you cross a germ and a comedian?

Sick jokes.

What do you get if you cross a comedian and a warm roll?

Hot cross puns.

What did Barbie, the play director, do when the actor playing Chicken Little forget his lines?

Barbie cued the chicken.

Why did Snoopy quit the comic strip?

He was tired of working for Peanuts.

Why wasn't the famous composer home?

He was out Chopin (shoppin').

Why was it hard to find the famous composer?

He was Haydn (hidin').

Why shouldn't you hit a famous composer?

He might hit you Bach (back).

What does a tuba call his father?

Ooom-papa.

What is the difference between sixteen ounces of lead and a pianist?

The lead weighs a pound and the pianist pounds away.

What number and letter sing at the opera?

10-R (tenor).

Did you hear the joke about the chocolate cake?
Never mind, it's too rich.

Did you hear the joke about the banana peel?
Sorry, it must have slipped my mind.

Did you hear the joke about the ice cube?
Never mind, it would only leave you cold.

Did you hear the joke about the garbage dump?
Never mind, it's a lot of rubbish.

Did you hear the joke about the tramp?
Never mind, it's a bummer.

Did you hear the joke about the branding iron?
Never mind, it's too hot to handle.

Did you hear the joke about the playing cards?
Never mind, it's no big deal.

Did you hear the joke about the sun?
Never mind, it's way over your head.

Did you hear the joke about the lion?
Never mind, it would only make you roar.

Did you hear the joke about the express train?
Never mind, you just missed it.

What song does a violinist sing to his violin?
  "I've got you under my chin. . . ."

What do you get if you cross a popular musician
and a shark?
  Rockjaw.

What part of your body has the most rhythm?
  Your eardrums.

Why did they let the turkey join the band?
  Because it had the drumsticks.

Why do people laugh at jokes about mountains?
Because they are hill-arious.

What reaction do you get when you tell stomach jokes?
Belly laughs.

What happens when you hear 1,000 Polish jokes?
They get Warsaw and Warsaw (worse-r and worse-r).

5. E-I-E-I-Oh!

How do chickens dance?
Chick-to-chick.

What is a hen's favorite vegetable?
Eggplant.

Every morning the farmer had eggs for breakfast.
He owned no chickens and he never got eggs from
anyone else's chickens. Where did he get his eggs?
From his ducks.

How do you begin a book about ducks?
With an intro-duck-tion.

Why do ducks have webbed feet?
To stamp out forest fires.

What time do ducks get up?
At the quack of dawn.

What kind of duck is a sharpshooter?
A quack shot.

What did the duck say when it fell in love with a
parrot?
"Quacker wants a polly."

What did the tree say to the woodchopper?
"Leaf me alone!"

Where do birds put their nests for safekeeping?
In a branch bank.

How much birdseed should you get for a quarter?
None. Quarters don't eat birdseed.

What kind of hawk has no wings?
A tomahawk.

What kind of geese are found in Portugal?
Portu-geese.

Why did the ram fall over the cliff?
It didn't see the ewe turn.

What do you get if you cross an octopus and a cow?
An animal that can milk itself.

What gives milk, goes "Moo, moo," and makes all your dreams come true?
Your Dairy Godmother.

Why did the cow jump over the moon?
Because the farmer had cold hands.

How did the cow jump over the moon?
She followed the Milky Way.

Why was the cow afraid?
Because she was a cow-ard.

When is the best time to milk a cow?
When she is in the moo-d.

What do you call a cow that can't give milk?
An udder failure.

Why don't cows ever have any money?
Because the farmer milks them dry.

Why is the letter K like a pig's tail?
Because it comes at the end of pork.

Why was the farmer angry?
Because someone got his goat.

What made the farmer yell?
Someone stepped on his corn.

Which bird is most worried about hygiene?
The rooster. He won't even lend anybody his comb.

How do you tell the difference between a rooster and a hen?
Throw the bird some seeds. If he eats it, it's a rooster; if she eats it, it's a hen.

What do you get if you cross a wolf and a rooster?
An animal that howls when the sun rises.

What do you get if you cross a chef and a rooster?
Cook-a-doodle-doo.

Why was the farmer arrested in the morning?
Because he hit the hay the night before.

You have four haystacks in one part of the field, seven in another and nine in the middle. You put them all together. How many do you have?
One, just one large haystack.

When does a farm go round and round?
When the farmer rotates his crops.

What happened when the farmer fell down the well?
He kicked the bucket.

Why did the silly farmer take a needle into the field?
To sow the corn.

After the autumn harvest there were nine ears of corn left in Farmer Smith's field. Each night a hungry rabbit sneaked into the field and took three ears home with him. How many nights did it take to get all the corn?
Nine nights. Two of the ears belonged to the rabbit.

What cuts lawns and gives milk?
A lawn moo-er.

When should a cow blow her horn?
When she's stuck in traffic.

What is most like a chicken stealin'?
A cock robin.

What size are very large eggs?
Eggs-tra large.

It takes three minutes to boil one egg. How long does it take to boil three eggs?
Three minutes.

If you saw a brown egg in a green box on a red table, where did it come from?
A chicken.

Where do blue Easter eggs come from?
Sad chickens.

Which is less intelligent—a large chicken or a small chicken?
The large one is the bigger cluck.

Why did the chicken sit on the axe?
So she could hatch-et.

What is the correct way to file an axe?
Under the letter A.

How do we know that owls are smarter than chickens?
Have you ever heard of Kentucky fried owl?

6. All Wet

What do you get when you cross a stream and a brook?

Wet feet.

What can you swallow that can also swallow you?
Water.

How does the earth fish?
With North and South Poles.

What geometric figure do sailors fear?
The Bermuda Triangle.

Why is the letter D like a sailor?
Because it follows the C (sea).

What is the difference between a timid child and a ship-wrecked sailor?
One clings to his ma, the other to his spar.

What kind of oven does the ocean use to cook its food?
Microwave.

Where is the ocean deepest?
On the bottom.

Why were the sardines out of work?
Because they got canned.

What do you get if you cross an owl with an oyster?
An animal that drops pearls of wisdom.

What happens when you ask an oyster a personal question?
It clams up.

How does a deaf fish hear?
With a herring aid.

What did one herring say to the other herring?
"Am I my brother's kipper?"

How does taking a ferry boat change people for the worse?
It makes them cross.

A man fell overboard from a ship in the middle of the ocean. He neither swam nor sank. How could that be?
He floated.

What does a ship weigh before it leaves port?
It weighs anchor.

What did the ship say to the pier?
"What's up, dock?"

What is the best way to cross a moat?
In a moat-er boat.

How do you catch an electric eel?
With a lightning rod.

What lives in the ocean, has eight legs and is quick on the draw?
Billy the Squid.

What does an octopus wear?
A coat of arms.

What would you get if you crossed an octopus and a mink?
You'd get a fur coat with too many sleeves.

What would you get if you crossed an octopus and a cat?
I don't know what you'd call it, but it would have eight arms and nine lives.

Why do some fishermen use helicopters to get their bait?

Because the whirly (early) bird gets the worm.

What is the favorite meal of a shipbuilder?

Launch.

Where is the best place to see a man-eating fish?

In a seafood restaurant.

What kind of fish do they serve on airplanes?

Flying fish.

What happens to a fish when it gets dizzy?
Its head swims.

What is quicker than a fish?
The one who catches it.

What part of a fish is like the end of a book?
The fin-is.

What do you get if you cross a kangaroo and a crocodile?
Leaping lizards.

What do you get if you cross a crocodile and an abalone?
You get a crocabalone (crock of baloney).

Where do they weigh whales?
At a whale weigh station.

What do whales like to chew?
Blubber gum.

Why did the whale cross the ocean?
To get to the other tide.

When does a wave beat the shore?
When it's fit to be tide (tied).

What did the beach say when the tide came in?
"Long time no sea."

7. Going Bananas

How do you make a hot dog stand?
Steal its chair.

Where do you find chili (chilly) beans?
At the North Pole.

When is a Chinese restaurant successful?
When it makes a fortune, cookie.

What is the difference between a zoo and a delicatessen?
A zoo has a man-eating tiger, and a delicatessen has a man eating salami.

What is the difference between a sharpshooter and a delicious meal?
One hits the mark; the other hits the spot.

What is the difference between the sun and a loaf of bread?
One rises from the east, the other from the yeast.

Why do bananas have to use suntan lotion?
Because bananas peel.

What did the peel say to the banana?
"Don't move, I've got you covered!"

What did the big grapefruit say to the little grapefruit?
"Come here, you little squirt!"

What did the big skillet say to the little skillet?
"Hi-ya, small fry!"

What did the doughnut say to the roll?
"If I had as much dough as you have, I wouldn't hang around this hole."

What is good on a roll but bad on a road?
Jam.

Who wears a crown, lives in a delicatessen, and calls for his fiddlers three?
Old King Cole Slaw.

Where do the people of India go for sandwiches?
To the New Delhi.

What is the quickest way to make soup taste terrible?
Change the U to an A, and you get soap.

What is orange and half a mile high?
The Empire State Carrot.

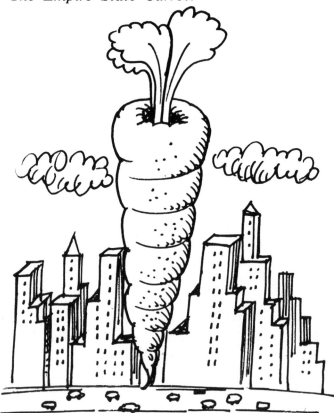

There are three tomatoes on a shelf. Two are ripe and one is green. Which one is the cowboy?
The green one. The other two are redskins.

What salad do people prefer when they want privacy?
Lettuce alone.

What is fat, green and goes "Oink, oink"?
Porky Pickle.

What is a pickle's all-time favorite musical?
"Hello, Dilly."

How do you spell pickle backwards?
P-I-C-K-L-E B-A-C-K-W-A-R-D-S.

What peels and chips but doesn't crack?
Potatoes.

How are potatoes like loyal friends?
They're always there when the chips are down.

What did one potato chip say to the other?
"Shall we go for a dip?"

What do sweet potatoes do when they play together?
They have yam sessions.

What do you get if you cross a potato and a sponge?
A vegetable that soaks up lots of gravy.

Why did the banana split?
Because it saw the bread box, the milk shake and the ginger snap.

How do you make meat loaf?
Send it on a holiday

What did Mary have for dinner?
Mary had a little lamb.

You have just eaten a meal made up of the side of a dead animal to which we feed waste, the unborn babies of a winged creature, and a weed that has been thrashed, baked and then burned. What meal of the day did you eat?
Breakfast. You just had bacon, eggs and toast.

What do termites eat for breakfast?
Oak meal.

What is three stories tall, green and tastes good on bread?
The Jelly Green Giant.

What snacks do robots serve at parties?
Assorted nuts.

What kind of nut has some of its inside outside?
A doughnut.

What do you get if you cross a doughnut and a pretzel?
A whole new twist.

What would you get if you stacked thousands of pizza pies on top of each other?
A leaning tower of pizza.

What is a pizza's favorite means of transportation?
Pie-cycle.

Where does the Gingerbread Man sleep?
Under a cookie sheet.

If cakes are 66 cents each, how much are upside-down cakes?
99 cents.

Why did the cook put the cake in the refrigerator?
Because she wanted icing on it.

How do you get pies to work for the government?
Add the letter S. It makes pies spies.

How many apples grow on a tree?
All of them.

If you took three apples from a basket that contained 13 apples, how many apples would you have?
If you took three apples, you'd have three apples.

What do you call 500 Indians without any apples?
The Indian apple-less 500.

What do you have when 134 strawberries try to get through the same door?
A strawberry jam.

What does a hungry mathematician like to eat?
A square meal.

Why should dieters avoid the letter C?
Because it makes fat a fact.

What illness do you get from overeating?
You get thick to your stomach.

8. So What?

What did the chocolate bar say to the lollipop?
"Hello, sucker!"

What did the pencil sharpener say to the pencil?
"Stop going around in circles and get to the point."

What did the protoplasm say to the amoeba?
"Don't bacilli!" (Don't be silly).

What is the difference between an animal losing its hair and a person painting a small building?
One sheds its coat; the other coats his shed.

What shampoo do mountains use?
Head and Boulders.

What did one hair say to the other hair?
"Don't you dare tangle with me!"

What is net profit?
What a fisherman earns.

Where do the nuts gather?
At the Hershey bar.

Who helped invent the telephone and had a cookie named after him?
Alexander Graham Cracker.

What mouse was ruler of the Romans?
Julius Cheeser (Caesar).

How can you make a moth ball?
Hit him with a fly swatter.

Which army officer is a pest?
A general nuisance.

What goes "Click, click, click, ouch!"?
A ball point sword.

What is red, white and blue, and handy if you have to sneeze?
Hanky Doodle Dandy.

How does a king open a door?
With a monarch-y.

How do you see King Arthur after it gets dark?
With a knight light.

What was Louis XIV chiefly responsible for?
Louis XV.

When is it impossible to give someone the time of day?
At night.

When is it good manners to spit in a man's face?
When his moustache is on fire.

What is E.T.'s favorite year?
19 E.T.-3 (1983).

Which is lighter, the sun or the earth?
The sun—it rises every morning.

Which continent is related to the Arctic Ocean?
Aunt-Arctica (Antarctica).

What do you need to spot an iceberg 20 miles away?
Good ice sight.

What did one raindrop say to the other?
"Two's company, three's a cloud."

What's wrong with letting a smile be your umbrella?
You end up with wet teeth.

If March winds bring April showers, and April showers bring May flowers, what do the May flowers bring?

Hayfever.

Why is doing nothing so tiring?

Because you can't stop and rest.

What are the odds of something happening at 12:50 P.M.?

Ten-to-one.

What weighs two tons, feels cold to the touch and comes on a stick?

A hippo-popsicle.

Do you have to be rich to ride in your own carriage?

Not if you're a baby.

Why can't a man living in New York City be buried west of the Mississippi?
Because he's still alive.

When is a person not a person?
When he's a little cross.

What is green and red all over?
A pickle holding its breath.

What is the pickle capital of the United States?
Dill-adelphia.

What is it like to have eight arms?
Very handy.

Why doesn't it pay to talk to anyone with four lips?
Because all you get is a lot of double talk.

What would you get if you crossed electric blankets with toasters?

People who pop out of bed in the morning.

Where can you buy a ruler that's three feet long?

At a yard sale.

What is the cheapest way to buy holes?

Wholesale.

What is the difference between a mailbox and a kangaroo?

If you don't know, remind me not to give you any letters to mail.

What do you get when you cross a woodpecker and a lion?

An animal that knocks before it eats you.

Why did the silly kid put his watch on the scale?

To see if it was gaining or losing time.

How do you keep a stupid person in suspense?

I'll tell you tomorrow.

9. World Records

What's faster than a speeding bullet, more powerful than a locomotive—and green?
Superpickle!

Which is the smartest pickle?
The one that uses its brine (brain).

$$\frac{E=Mc^2}{\sqrt{X-4}}$$

$$\sum_{\infty}^{o}$$

Who was the most brilliant pig in the world?
Ein-swine.

Which letters are the smartest?
The Y's (wise).

Who are the slowest talkers in the world?
Convicts—they can spend 25 years on a single sentence.

What is the saddest piece of clothing?
Blue jeans.

What is the saddest picture?
A blueprint.

What door is the saddest?
A revolving door, because everyone is always pushing it around.

What is the oldest fruit?
Adam's apple.

Who was the straightest man in the Bible?
Joseph, because Pharaoh made him a ruler.

Did you hear about the highest paid acrobat in the world?
He flies through the air with the greatest of fees.

Who is the best contortionist in the world?
The sailor who sits on his chest.

What is the best-looking geometric figure?
Acute angle.

What beam weighs the least?
A moon beam.

What is the most noble creature of the sea?
The Prince of Whales (Wales).

What is the most popular gardening magazine?
"The Weeder's (Reader's) Digest."

10. Home Sweet Home

What does a troll call his apartment?
Gnome sweet gnome.

What is purple and a member of your family?
Your grape grandmother.

What kind of screen brings things into the house instead of keeping them out?
A television screen.

Why was the house empty?
Because the fire went out; the steam escaped; the rope skipped; the eggs scrambled; the milk evaporated; the scissors cut out; and the stockings ran.

When is a house not on land nor on water?
When it's on fire.

What room has no walls, no doors, no windows and no floors?
A mushroom.

How many bricks does it take to finish a house?
Only one—the last one.

What pillar is never used to hold up a building?
A caterpillar.

Can February March?
No, but April May.

What do canaries say on Halloween?
"Twick or tweet!"

What did Adam say on the day before Christmas?
"It's Christmas, Eve."

What does Tarzan sing at Christmas time?
"Jungle Bells."

What is green and sour and gives presents at Christmas time?
Santapickle.

What goes "Ho, ho, ho, swoosh, ho, ho, ho, swoosh"?
Santa Claus caught in a revolving door.

What do you have in December that you don't have in any other month?
The letter D.

Who isn't your sister and isn't your brother, but is still a child of your mother and father?
You.

If a father gave his son 19 cents and his daughter 6 cents, what time would it be?
A quarter to two.

Why do your uncles, aunts and cousins depend on you?
Because without U, your uncles, aunts and cousins couldn't exist.

How many relatives went to the picnic?
Three uncles and 100,000 ants.

What plants are the most greedy?
Weeds. Give them an inch and they'll take a yard.

Why did the rich parents keep their son in the refrigerator?
So he wouldn't get spoiled.

If a mouse ran out of your stove and you had a
gun, could you shoot it?
No, it would be out of your range.

What do you get when you use soap and water on
the stove?
Foam on the range.

What invention allows people to walk through
walls?
Doors.

Can you make one word from the letters of "new
door"?
Yes—"one word."

How can you touch the floor without standing on
your feet or hands?
Fall out of bed.

What is the difference between someone going up
the stairs and someone looking up?
*One steps up the stairs, the other stares up
the steps.*

Why did the foolish man wring his hands?
Because his bell was out of order.

What did the ceiling say to the four walls?
"Hold me up, I'm plastered."

What stays indoors no matter how many times you put it out?

The light.

What could cause a lot of trouble if it stopped smoking?

A chimney.

What did the digital watch say to its mother?

"Look, Ma, no hands!"

Why is the letter D so aggravating?

Because it makes ma mad.

When the baby cries at night, who gets up?

The whole neighborhood.

What were Alexander Graham Bell's first words?

"Goo-goo."

11. Oops!

What is stucco?
What you get when you sit on gummo.

What did the lumberjack shout when the tree fell too soon?
"Tim . . ."

What do you get if you cross an earthquake and a forest fire?
Shake and bake.

What do you get if you cross a train going 80 miles an hour and an auto going 55 miles an hour?
A BIG funeral.

An airplane, flying from the United States to Canada, crashed right on the border between the two countries. Where would they bury the survivors—in Canada or in the United States?
Neither. They don't bury survivors.

How can you fall from the Empire State Building and not get hurt?
Fall from the front step.

What happened to the man who took a 100-foot dive into a glass of root beer?

Nothing. It was a soft drink.

What swings through the trees and has purple juice smeared all over his body?

Tarzan of the Grapes.

What were Tarzan's last words?

"Who greased the vine?"

Why did the angry man put a firecracker under his pancakes?

He wanted to blow his stack.

What does a match do when it loses its temper?

It flares up.

How do soldiers sleep out in the open?
In beds of flowers, under sheets of rain and blankets of fog.

What loses its head every morning but gets it back at night?
A pillow.

What pierces your ears without leaving a hole?
Noise.

What caused the riot in the post office?
A stampede.

What has 400 teeth and says "Beware of the dog"?

A picket fence with a sign on it.

What would happen if you cut your left side off?

You'd be all right.

What happened when the pelican stuck his head into the wall socket?

He got an electric bill.

What does the voice of experience say?

"Ouch!"

What is green and long and grouchy?

A sour pickle.

What does a banana do when it sees a gorilla?

The banana splits.

What happened to the peanut that was mugged?

It was assaulted (a-salted).

Why did the worm oversleep?

It didn't want to be caught by the early bird.

When are you neither left-handed nor right-handed?

When you are underhanded.

What could you get if you fell on a phonograph record?

A slipped disc.

What happens when you slip on thin ice?

Your backside gets thaw.

71

What happened when the nail had a fight with the tire?

The nail knocked it flat.

What did the nail say to the hammer?

"Why don't you hit someone your own size?"

What is the difference between a pitchfork and a toothpick?

Well, if you don't know, better not pick your teeth.

What is worse than being with a fool?

Fooling with a bee.

What kind of bee can't make up its mind?

A may-bee.

What kind of bee drops its honey?

A spilling (spelling) bee.

What kind of bee hums and drops things?

A fumble bee.

How do bees go to school?

They take the buzz (bus).

What kind of gum do bees chew?

Bumble gum.

What is a bee's favorite song?

"Bee it ever so humble, there's no place like comb. . . ."

12. Love & Kisses

What did the letter say to the postage stamp?
"You send me."

What did the stamp say when it fell in love with the envelope?
"I'm stuck on you."

What did the phonograph needle say to the record?
"Care to go for a spin?"

What do roses call each other?
"Bud-dy."

What do squirrels give each other on Valentine's Day?
Forget-me-nuts.

What do you get if you cross an absent-minded professor with an insect?
A forget-me-gnat.

Did you hear about the girl who was engaged to a fellow with a wooden leg?
Her father broke it off.

Why was the light bulb interested in the light switch?
It turned him on.

What would you get if Ferdinand the Bull married Liza Minnelli?
You'd get Ferdiliza (fertilizer).

What can turn a lad into a lady?
The letter Y.

Why does Lucy like the letter K?
It makes Lucy lucky.

A doctor and a bus driver were in love with the same woman. The bus driver had to go away for a week, so he gave the woman seven apples. Why?
Because an apple a day keeps the doctor away.

Who are the best letter-writers?
Fishermen. They'll always drop you a line.

What are the best letters to read in hot weather?
Fan mail.

What is green and sour and always changing its mind?
A fickle pickle.

74

Why was Adam's first day so long?
There was no Eve.

What did the boy snake say to the girl snake?
"Give me a little hiss."

What happened when the couple tried to kiss in the dense fog?
They mist.

How do you kiss a hockey player?
You pucker up.

How do you send a message to a Viking?
  By Norse code.

What part of the body has the best social life?
  The tonsils, because they get taken out so often.

Whose figure can't you see?
  A figure of speech.

If two cows helped each other, what would that be?
  Cow-operation.

Why did the banana go out with the prune?
Because it couldn't get a date.

Who do mermaids date?
They go out with the tide.

What did the tube of toothpaste say to the toothbrush?
"Give me a squeeze and I'll meet you outside."

What did the little hand·say to the big hand?
"Meet me at noon for lunch."

What did Cleopatra say when Mark Antony asked if she was true to him?
"Omar Khayyam (Oh, Mark, I am)."

13. Greetings!

How do retired sailors greet each other?
   "Long time no sea."

How do surfers greet each other?
   "Hawaii (How are you), sport?"

How do clocks greet each other?
   "Hour (How are) you doing?"

How do scarecrows greet each other?
  "Hay, man!"

How do real estate agents greet each othe ?
  "House (how's) business?"

How do soldiers greet each other?
  "How warrior (are you)?"

How do midgets greet each other?
  "Small world, isn't it?"

How do angels greet each other?
  "Halo, there!"

79

How does an electric rabbit greet you?
It says, "Watts up, Doc?"

How do you greet a web-footed bird?
You say, "What's up, duck?"

How did the near-sighted beaver greet the return-
ing weasel?
"Welcome back, otter."

How did the rake greet the hoe?
"Hi, hoe!"

How do Martian cowboys greet each other?
With communication saddle lights (satellites).

14. What's Your Line?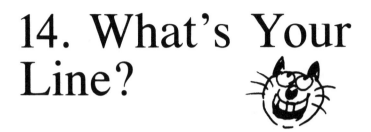

If a gardener has a green thumb, who has a purple thumb?

A near-sighted plumber.

Who gets congratulated when they're down and out?

Astronauts.

What kind of case would a lawyer have if he slipped and hurt himself at the pool?

A bathing suit.

Why did the baker bring a wheel into his bakery?

He wanted to roll in dough.

Why do bakers always want dough?

Because they knead it.

What is a banker's favorite dance?

The vaults (waltz).

Why do bankers go to art school?

They like to draw interest.

What well-known band leader collected $100,000 in one minute?
Jesse James.

Why was the bowlegged cowboy fired?
Because he couldn't get his calves together.

How do you find a missing barber?
Comb the city.

What do you call a carpenter who misplaces his tools?
A saw loser.

How did the ditch digger get his job?
He just fell into it.

What is an electrician's favorite ice cream?
Shock-a-lot.

What do they call an Alaskan eyeglass fitter?
An optical Aleutian (illusion).

Who grows the cucumbers for a pickle factory?
The farmer in the dill.

Why did the candy factory hire the farmer's daughter?
They needed someone to milk chocolates.

Why can't you trust fishermen and shepherds?
Because they live by hook and by crook.

What is the difference between a gardener and a laundryman?
One keeps the lawn wet, the other keeps the laun-dry.

What kind of chair does a geologist like to relax on?
A rock-ing chair.

Where do geologists go for entertainment?
To rock concerts.

Why did the knife sharpener quit his job?
He couldn't take the grind.

Why did the silly kid put his head on the grind-stone?

To sharpen his wits.

What is a minister doing when he rehearses his sermon?

Practicing what he preaches.

What person makes a living by talking to himself?

A ventriloquist.

Where do pilots keep their personal belongings?

In air pockets.

What month is worst for soldiers?

A long March.

What do you call the boss at a dairy?
The big cheese.

How do tailors feel when they are neither happy nor unhappy?
Sew-sew.

What do tailors do when they get tired?
They press on.

A night watchman was in a stable guarding the owner's prize horse. One night he dreamed the horse was run over by a train. He told the owner it was a sign that something bad would happen to the horse. What did the owner do? He fired the night watchman. Why?
The night watchman was sleeping on the job.

Who works the late shift in a pajama factory?
The nightie watchman.

Why was the weather forecaster arrested?
For shooting the breeze.

When are lumberjacks busiest?
Sep-timmmmmber!

15. Peculiar Pets

What color is a happy cat?
Purr—ple.

How do you get milk from a cat?
Steal its saucer.

How is cat food sold?
So much purr can.

Why did the silly kid try to feed pennies to the cat?
Because his mother told him to put money in the kitty.

What is a cat's favorite dessert?
Mice (rice) pudding.

What do you get if you cross a hungry cat and a canary?
A cat that isn't hungry any more.

What do you call someone who steals cats?
A purr-snatcher.

What is the difference between a cat and a puss?
I like your cat—but not your puss!

"I guarantee," said the salesman in the pet shop, "that this parrot will repeat every word it hears." The customer bought the bird. When he took the parrot home, however, the parrot would not utter a single word. Nevertheless, what the salesman said was true. How could that be?

The parrot was deaf.

What do you get if you cross a shark and a parrot?

An animal that talks your ear off.

What do you get if you cross a parrot and a woodpecker?

A bird that talks to you in Morse code.

What do you get if you cross a parrot and a homing pigeon?

A bird that asks the way home if it gets lost.

What do you get if you cross a parrot and a duck?

A bird that says, "Polly wants a quacker."

What do you call it when five toads sit on top of each other?

A toad-em pole.

What is the difference between a dog and a marine scientist?

One wags a tail, the other tags a whale.

When is a dog's tail not a dog's tail?

When it is a waggin' (wagon).

What do you call the last three hairs of a dog's tail?

Dog hairs.

What is green and thin and jumps every few seconds?

Asparagus with hiccups.

What is green and makes a noise you can hear for miles?

A frog horn.

What is a frog's favorite flower?

Crocus.

Why doesn't a frog jump when it's sad?

It's too unhoppy.

What is the difference between a frog and a cat?

A frog croaks all the time, a cat only nine times.

What would you get if you crossed a noisy frog and a shaggy dog?

A croaker spaniel.

What flower do you get if you cross a pointer and a setter?
A poinsettia.

What happens to a dog who eats table scraps?
He gets splinters in his tongue.

What dog do you find at the U.N.?
A diplo-mutt.

Where do they send homeless dogs?
To an arf-anage.

What do you get if you cross a Pekingese and a Pomeranian?
A peeking pom (peeping Tom).

What kind of pet did Aladdin have?
A flying car-pet.

What is stormy weather for mice and rats?
When it rains cats and dogs.

What big cat lives in the backyard?
A clothes lion.

What person delivers mail for cats?
A litter carrier.

What is cat fur?
Fur chasing mice.

What happened when the cat swallowed a ball of yarn?
She had mittens.

What goes "Dit-dit-dot croak, dit-dit-dot croak?"
Morse toad.

What do you use to catch baby frogs with?
Tadpoles.

What would happen if you illegally parked a frog?
It would get toad (towed) away.

What did the frog say to the tailor who couldn't find the scissors?
"Rippit! Rippit!"

What do you say to a hitch-hiking frog?
"Hop in!"

16. School Daze

What is big and yellow and comes in the morning to brighten Mother's day?
The school bus.

On the school door was a sign that said, "Please Do Not Knock Before Entering." What kind of school was it?
A karate school.

A class has a top and a bottom. What lies in between?
The student body.

Why shouldn't you mention the number 288 in front of the principal?
Because it is two (too) gross. (A gross is 144.)

Why did the teacher excuse the little firefly?
Because when you've got to glow, you've got to glow.

What did the professor say as his glass eye slid down the drain?
"I guess I've lost another pupil."

What does an elf do when it gets home from school?

Gnomework.

Where's the best place to find books about trees?
A branch library.

Why wasn't the clock allowed in the library?
It tocked too much.

Why are clocks always tired?
You would be too if you had to run all day.

Why was the clock scratching?
Because it had ticks.

What time is it when it's halfway between the "tick" and the "tock"?

Half-past ticks o'tock.

What kind of poetry can you make up out of your head?

Blank verse.

Why is the pen mightier than the sword?

Because no one has yet invented a ballpoint sword.

What was Samuel Clemens' pen name?
He never had a name for his pen.

What is NBC?
A dumb way to start the alphabet.

How many letters are there in the alphabet?
24—E.T. went home.

What word has three double letters in a row?
Bookkeeper.

How do you make the word "one" disappear?
Put a G at the beginning and it's "gone."

What do you find more in sorrow than in anger?
The letter R.

This paragraph looks so ordinary that you would think that nothing was wrong with it at all, and, in fact, nothing is. But it is unusual. Why? If you study it and think about it, you may find out, but I am not going to assist you in any way. You must do it without any coaching. No doubt, if you work at it for long it will dawn on you—who knows? Go to work now and try your skill!
There is no E in the paragraph.

Why was the little bird punished in school?
It was caught peeping during a test.

What is the best way to improve a long speech?
Use shortening.

Len has it before. Paul has it behind. Bryan never had it at all. Ralph has it once. All girls have it once. Boys can't have it. Old Mrs. Mulligan has it twice in succession. Dr. Lowell has it twice as bad at the end as in the beginning. What is it?

The letter L.

What happens when you throw a red rock in the Black Sea?

It goes, "Kerplunk!"

A box is filled with water. It weighs 1,000 pounds. What can you add to make it weigh less?

Holes.

How is it possible for John to stand in back of Tom while Tom stands in back of John?

Have them stand back to back.

What's in the church?
But not in the steeple?
The parson has it,
But not the people.

The letter R.

What is the best way to pass a geometry test?

Know all the angles.

What geometric figure is always correct?

A right angle.

What is the difference between shillings and pence?

You can walk down the street without shillings.

Tim said to Jim, "Give me a dollar, and then I'll have as much as you." Jim said to Tim, "No, you give me a dollar, and then I'll have twice as much as you." How much did each one have?

Tim had five dollars; Jim had seven.

How many feet are there in the world?

Twice as many as there are people.

A man was offered a coin imprinted with the date 1200 B.C. He refused to buy it. Why?

How could the date B.C. be on the coin 1200 years before Christ was born? The coin had to be a fraud.

What can you find in the Great Wall of China that the Chinese never put there?

Cracks.

Rick and Dick were leaving the cafeteria. As they passed the cashier, Rick paid his bill, but Dick handed the cashier a slip of paper with the number 1004180 on it. The cashier studied the number for a moment, then let Dick pass by without paying. Why?

The number 1004180 reads: "I owe nothing, for I ate nothing."

It takes 12 one-cent stamps to make a dozen. How many six-cent stamps does it take to make a dozen?

It takes 12 of anything to make a dozen, even six-cent stamps.

Where is Timbuktu?
Between Timbuk-one and Timbuk-three.

What is raised during the rainy season in Brazil?
Umbrellas.

If George Washington were alive today, what would he be most famous for?
Old age.

17. Sick & Tired

Why wasn't Eve afraid of getting the mumps?
Because she'd Adam.

What stretcher can't carry sick people?
A rubber band.

Why did the surgeon wear a tuxedo in the operating room?
Because he always dressed formally for an opening.

Who performs the operations in a fish hospital?
The head sturgeon.

How long should doctors practice medicine?
Until they get it right.

What goes "Chit-chat, tick-tock, boom-bang"?
A sick clock.

Where does a watchmaker take his sick watches?
To the tick doc.

What sickness can't you talk about until it's cured?

Laryngitis.

What is the difference between a sick sailor and a blind man?

One can't go to sea; the other can't see to go.

How much does a psychiatrist charge an elephant?

$50 for the visit and $500 for the couch.

What did Old MacDonald see on the eye chart?

E-I-E-I-O.

What does a dentist say when you enter his office?
"Gum on in!"

Why didn't the dentist laugh at the joke about the sore tooth?
Because he hurt (heard) that one before.

What is the difference between a lion with a toothache and a rainy day?
One roars with pain; the other pours with rain.

What is the difference between a New Yorker and a dentist?
One roots for the Yanks; the other yanks for the roots.

What kind of teeth can you buy for a dollar?
Buck teeth.

Why didn't the silly kid want to use toothpaste?
Because his teeth weren't loose.

Why shouldn't you brush your teeth with gun powder?
You might shoot your mouth off.

Why did the silly dentist throw out his electric toothbrush?
Because none of his patients had electric teeth.

How do you straighten crooked apple trees?
You send them to an orchardontist (orthodontist).

Why can't you believe what a doctor says?
Because he makes MD (empty) promises.

What is the best way to avoid wrinkles?
Don't sleep in your clothes.

What is the best thing for nail biting?
Sharp teeth.

What is the difference between a rug and a bottle of medicine?
One you take up and shake, the other you shake up and take.

What bee is good for your health?
Vitamin B.

What should you do if you find yourself with water on the knee, water on the elbow, and water on the brain?
Turn off the shower.

Where do backpackers keep sleeping pills?
In their knapsacks (nap sacks).

What do you give an elk with indigestion?
Elk-A-Seltzer.

What happens when corn catches cold?
It gets an ear ache.

What paper is most like a sneeze?
Tissue!

Where is a sneeze usually pointed?
Atchoo!

Why did the house call for a doctor?
Because it had window panes.

Where do you send a sick pony?
To the horse-pital.

What disease does grass get?
Hay fever.

How can you tell if your lawn is sick?
When you hear the grass mown (moan).

What did one escalator say to the other escalator?
"I think I'm coming down with something."

What do you get if a dinosaur steps on your foot?
Anklosaurus.

What do you get if you cross poison ivy with a four-leaf clover?
You get a rash of good luck.

What happens when the sun gets tired?
It sets a while.

Why was Mickey Mouse always falling down?
Because he had Disney spells.

18. Sports Can Be Funny

What did one bicycle wheel say to the other?
"Was it you who spoke?"

Which book tells you everything you want to know about bicycles?
A bicycl-opedia.

What do you get if you tie two bicycles together?
Siamese Schwinns.

Why are fish poor tennis players?
Because they don't like to get close to the net.

What soccer player is never promoted?
The left back.

How is it possible for you to go down from the top of a mountain without first going up?
Be born at the top.

What is the difference between a race horse and a locomotive?

One is trained to run; the other runs a train.

Why is a leaking faucet like a horse race?
It's off and running.

If two shirt collars had a race, who would win?
Neither. It would end in a tie.

What did you need to win a race in the old Roman Colosseum?
Faith, hope and chariot.

What is the favorite sport of an executioner?
Sleighing (slaying).

What do you have when there is no snow?
Tough sledding.

Why is it hard to drive a golf ball?
Because it doesn't have a steering wheel.

Why did the sports fan spend so much time in the bathroom?
He likes to watch the toilet bowl.

Why did the bowling pins lie down?
Because they were on strike.

When do boxers start wearing gloves?
When the weather gets cold.

What bird is useful in boxing matches?
Duck.

Why did the match box?
Because it saw the ski jump, the wood fence, and the fruit punch.

What has 22 legs and goes crunch, crunch, crunch?
A football team eating potato chips.

Where do they serve snacks to football players?
In the Soup-er Bowl.

If two flies went into the kitchen, which one would be the football player?
The one in the sugar bowl.

What is the difference between a football player and a duck?
One you find in a huddle, the other in a puddle.

What three R's do cheerleaders have to learn?
Rah! Rah! Rah!

Why was Cinderella such a poor football player?
Because she had a pumpkin for a coach.

Why didn't the first baseman get to dance with Cinderella?
Because he missed the ball.

What has 18 legs, red spots, and catches flies?
A baseball team with measles.

When was baseball first mentioned in the Bible?
In the first line: "In the big inning. . . ."

What do you call a baseball hit high in the air during a game played under lights?
A fly-by-night.

Why was the baseball player asked to come along on the camping trip?
They needed someone to pitch the tent.

Why do bakers make good baseball pitchers?
Because they know their batter.

Why was the piano tuner hired to play on the baseball team?
Because he had perfect pitch.

What would you get if Betty Crocker married a baseball player?
Better batter.

What is the difference between a baseball umpire and a pickpocket?
An umpire watches steals, a pickpocket steals watches.

Why don't baseball players join unions?
Because they don't like to be called out on strikes.

What do baseball players on third base like to sing?
"There's no place like home."

Why didn't anyone drink soda pop at the double-header baseball game?
Because the home team lost the opener.

Why did the umpire throw the chicken out of the baseball game?
He suspected fowl play.

What serious traffic violation is allowed in baseball?
Hit-and-run.

What would you get if you crossed a basketball with a newborn snake?
You'd get a bouncing baby boa.

How are judges like basketball referees?
They both work the courts.

Why are basketball coaches happy?
Because they whistle while they work.

What do you call a six-foot-tall basketball player?
Shortie.

What kind of match won't light fires?
A wrestling match.

What kind of running means walking?
Running out of gas.

Where should a jogger wash his sneakers?
In running water.

Why did the long distance runner go to the veterinarian?
Because his calves hurt.

19. Going Crazy

How can you avoid being driven crazy?
Walk.

What is the funniest car on the road?
A Jolkswagen.

Do Cadillacs stretch?
No, but Mercedes Benz.

What kind of car do toads drive?
Hop rods.

What is black and wrinkled and makes pit stops?
A racing prune.

What was the tow truck doing at the auto race?
Trying to pull a fast one.

What is a good license plate for a racing car?
XLR8.

What flies without wings, propellers or jets?
Time.

Why does time fly?
To get away from all the people who are trying to kill it.

How do you get a mouse to fly?
Buy it an airline ticket.

What kind of train has no wheels?
A train of thought.

Glendale and Springdale are at each end of a railroad track 100 miles long. At exactly the same instant, one train leaves Glendale and one leaves Springdale. The engineer operating the train from Glendale averages 50 miles an hour, while the engineer on the train from Springdale averages 40 miles an hour. Where will they meet?
In the hospital.

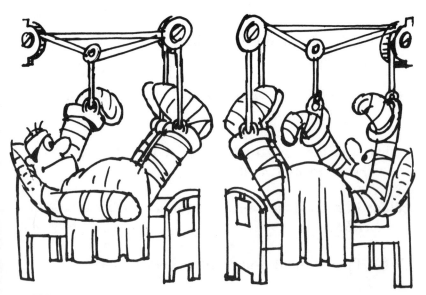

What has eight wheels but carries only one passenger?
A pair of roller skates.

Why is a boat the cheapest form of transportation?
Because it runs on water.

How do you top a car?
Tep on the brake, toopid!

What kind of car is best to drive in the fall?
An autumn-mobile.

What kind of car do movie stars wish for?
An Os-car.

What kind of car do rich rock stars drive?
A Rock and Rolls-Royce.

Why did the motorist put a rabbit in his gas tank?
Because he needed the car for short hops.

How do you charge a battery?
With a credit card.

Why did the garage mechanic wear a disguise?
Because he wanted to be a secret service man.

What kind of shot do you give a sick car?
A fuel injection.

What makes a road broad?
The letter B.

What do you call an elephant hitchhiker?
A two-and-a-half ton pickup.

What do you get if you cross a rhinoceros and a goose?
An animal that honks before it runs you over.

Which traffic light is the bravest?
The one that doesn't turn yellow.

A man rides on horseback from New York City to Virginia. The trip normally takes four days. He leaves New York on Wednesday and arrives on the same Wednesday. How could he do this?
His horse is named Wednesday.

What is green and goes slam, slam, slam, slam?
A four-door pickle.

20. Monstermania

Why wouldn't the vampire climb back into his coffin at sunrise?
He was an all-day sucker.

If two vampires had a race, who would win?
Neither. They would finish neck and neck.

What would you get if you crossed a vampire bat and a magician?
A flying sorcerer.

What does an up-to-date witch fly?
An electric broom.

How does a witch travel when she doesn't have a broom?
She witch-hikes.

What is a little zombie's favorite stuffed animal?
Its deady bear.

What game do little ghouls like to play?
Corpse and Robbers.

How does the Abominable Snowman get around?
By icicle (bicycle).

What is the first thing little vampires learn in school?
The alpha-bat.

What is a two-headed monster's favorite ball game?
A double-header.

What would you get if you crossed the Frankenstein monster and a hot dog?
A Frankfurterstein.

If the Frankenstein monster and a werewolf jumped off the Empire State Building, who would land first?
Who cares?

118

What is a monster's favorite holiday?
April Ghoul's Day.

What is on the cover of a monster beauty magazine?
A cover ghoul.

What law do all ghouls follow?
The Law of Grave-ity.

What is a monster's normal eyesight?
20–20–20–20–20.

How does a monster predict the future?
With a horrorscope.

Where does a monster keep an extra set of arms?
In a hand bag.

What happened to the woman who covered herself with vanishing cream?
Nobody knows.

What kind of children would the Invisible Man and Woman have?
I don't know, but they wouldn't be much to look at.

What do you call the sweetheart of a ghoul?
A ghoul friend.

What is the most important thing you need to be to be a zombie?
Dead.

What is Count Dracula's favorite flavor of ice cream?
Vein-illa.

What is a shark's favorite ice cream?
There are several: finalla, jawberry, shark-olate and toothy fruity.

What is the soft, mushy stuff between a shark's teeth?
Slow swimmers.

What did the Martian say to the gas pump?
"Take your finger out of your ear and listen to me!"

What is a witch's favorite breakfast?
Scrambled hex.

How do ghosts like their eggs?
Terri-fried.

What flowers do monsters grow?
Mari-ghouls and mourning gorys.

What did the monster eat after the dentist pulled its tooth?
The dentist.

What gets 25 miles to a gallon of plasma?
A bloodmobile.

What is the best way to see flying saucers?
Pinch the waitress.

What should a monster do when it gets a sore throat?

Gar-goyle (gargle).

Did you hear about the latest Dr. Jekyll and Mr. Hyde miracle medicine?

One sip and you're a new man.

What comes from outer space and leads a parade?

A Martian band.

What do you call it when demons get together in a rally?

A demon-stration.

What is the best way to get rid of a demon?
Exorcise a lot.

Why did the fat ghost go on a strict diet?
It wanted to keep its ghoulish figure.

Who do vampires invite to family reunions?
Blood relations.

Why did Dracula go to the orthodontist?
To improve his bite.

What kind of coffee does Dracula drink when he gets out of his casket?
De-coffin-ated coffee.

What do you get when you cross Dracula and a knight?

A bite in shining armor.

What is the first safety rule for witches?

Don't fly off the handle.

How do you tell a dinosaur to hurry?

You say, "Shake a lego-saurus!"

Who is a little dinosaur's favorite baby-sitter?

Ty-granny-saurus rex.

What business is King Kong in?

Monkey business.

What should you do if you meet King Kong?

Give him a BIG banana.

What do you say to King Kong when he gets married?

Kongratulations!

What kind of parts did Dracula get when he went to Hollywood?

Bit parts.

What drink is popular among monsters?

Ghoul-aid.

Where do ghosts pick up their mail?

At the ghost office.

What do you get when you cross a ghost and an elephant?

A big nothing.

Why did the elephant cross the road?

Because he didn't want to hear that last joke.

What did one mummy say to the other when they left each other?

"B.C.'ing you!"

Index

Aardvark, 5
Abalone, 45
Abominable Snowman, 118
Absentmindedness, 73
Acrobat, 61,
Adam, 64, 75, 100
Adam's apple, 61
Age, 99
Airline ticket, 114
Airplanes, 44, 68
Aladdin, 90
Alaska, 83
Alphabet, 95, 118
Amoeba, 53
Angels, 79
Anger, 95
Animal: riddles, 5–13;
  stuffed, 117
Animals, 27
Ants, 65
Apartment, 63
Apes, 12
Apples, 52, 74
Apple trees, 103
Arctic Ocean, 55
Arms, 57, 119
Arthur, King, 55
Art school, 81
Asparagus, 89
Astronauts, 81
Axe, 40

Baby, 56, 67; sitter, 123
Bach, 31
Backpackers, 104
Backside, 71
Baker, 81, 110
Ball, 26, 109; games, 109-112,
  118
Banana, 7,30, 477, 71, 77,
  123; peel, 32; split, 50, 71
Band, 33; leader, 82;
  Martian, 121; rubber, 100
Band-aid, 26
Bank, 36
Bankers, 81
Barber, 82
Baseball, 109, 110, 111
Basketball, 111, 112
Bathing suit, 81
Battery, 115
Beach, 45
Bear, 12
Beaver, 80
Bed, 11, 66, 70
Bee, 72, 103

Bell, 66; Alexander
  Graham, 67
Belt, 20
Bermuda Triangle, 41
Bible, 61, 109
Bicycle, 106
Bill, electric, 71
Bird: early, 71; seed, 36
Birds, 36, 38, 80, 95
Black Sea, 96
Blankets, 70; electric, 58
Blind man, 101
Bloodmobile, 120
Blueprint, 60
Boat, 115
Book, 24, 45, 106
Bookkeeper, 95
Bowling, 108
Box, 96
Boxers, 108
Boxing, 109
Brains, 59
Branding iron, 32
Brazil, 99
Bread: box, 50; loaf of, 46
Breakfast, 23, 35, 50, 120
Bricks, 64
Brook, 41
Broom, electric, 117
Building, 64
Burglar, 19
Burial, 57, 68
Bus, 72

Cadillacs, 113
Caesar, Julius, 54
Cafeteria, 98
Cakes, 32, 51, 52
Calves, 82, 112
Camel, 9
Camping trip, 110
Canada, 68; Dry, 30
Canaries, 64, 86
Candy, 22; factory, 83
Capital, 99
Cards, playing, 14, 25, 26,
  32
Carpenter, 82
Carriage, 56
Carrot, 48
Cars, 113, 115
Caterpillar, 64
Cats, 43, 86, 89, 90
Ceiling, 66
Cement mixer, 20
Cereal, 23
Chair, 83
Chariot, 107
Cheerleaders, 109
Chef, 38
Chess, 26
Chicken, 13, 23, 40, 111;
  Little, 31; see Hen

Child, 41
Children, 119
Chili, 46
Chimney, 67
Chimpanzees, 11
China, 98
Chinese restaurant, 46
Chocolates, 83
Chopin, 31
Christmas, 64, 65
Cinderella, 109
Cities, 14
Class, 92
Clemens, Samuel, 95
Cleopatra, 77
Clock, 77, 78, 93, 100; see
  Watch
Clothes, 14-18, 60, 103
Coaches, 109, 112
Coat, 53
Code, 76
Coffee, 29, 122
Cokes, 30
Cold, 76, 104
Collie, 26
Colosseum, 107
Combs, 9, 38
Comedians, 14, 23, 24, 25,
  30, 31
Comic strip, 14, 31
Composer, 31
Contortionist, 62
Convicts, 60
Cookie, 54
Corn, 37, 39, 97, 104
Couch, 101
Counterfeit money, 21
Courts, 112
Cow, 36, 37, 39, 76
Coward, 36
Cowboys, 49, 82; Martian,
  80
Credit card, 115
Crime, 19-22
Crocker, Betty, 110
Crocodile, 45
Crocus, 89
Crops, 39
Croquet, 23
Cucumbers, 83

Dairy, 85
Dancing, 26, 27, 35, 81
Dates, 77
Day, first, 75
DDT, 21
December, 65
Delicatessen, 46
Demons, 121, 122
Dentist, 102, 103, 120
Dessert, 86
Detectives, 20
Diet, 52, 122

125

Dinosaur, 105, 123
Disc, slipped, 71
Disease, 104
Disguise, 115
Disney, 105
Ditch digger, 83
Dive, 69
Doctor, 74, 100, 103, 104
Dogs, 16, 71, 89, 90
Donkeys, 12
Door, 60, 66; *see Revolving door*
Double talk, 57
Doughnut, 47, 50
Dracula, 120, 122, 123
Dresser, 17
Dressmaker, 14
Drink, popular, 123
Duck, 15, 35, 88, 108, 109

Ear: ache, 104; drum, 33
Early bird, 71
Ears, 70
Earth, 41, 55
Earthquake, 68
Easter eggs, 40
Eel, 43
Eggplant, 35
Eggs, 24, 35, 40, 50, 63, 120
Electrician, 83
Elephants, 6, 7, 8, 9, 10, 13, 17, 21, 25, 101, 116, 124
Elf, 93
Elk, 104
Empire State Building, 12, 68, 118
Engagement, 74
Envelope, 73
Escalator, 104
E.T., 55, 95
Eve, 64, 75, 100
Executioner, 107
Experience, 71
Eye: glass, 92; glasses, 21; sight, 119

Fall, 68
Family, 65; reunions, 122
Fan mail, 74
Farmer, 35, 36, 37, 39, 83
Fat, 52, 122
Faucet, 107
February, 64
Feet, 97
Fence, 109; picket, 71
Ferdinand the Bull, 74
Ferry boat, 42
Figures, 62, 76, 96, 122
Fire, 63, 112; cracker, 69; fly, 15, 92; forest, 68
Fishermen, 44, 53, 83
Fishes, 23, 42, 44, 45, 106
Fish hospital, 100
Fishing, 41

Flies, 109
Floodlights, 25
Floor, 66
Flowers, 89, 120
Flute, 26
Flying: carpet, 90; saucers, 120
Fool, 72
Football, 109
Fortune: cookie, 46; teller, 26
Four-leaf clover, 105
Frankenstein monster, 118
Frankfurter, 20
Friends, 49
Frogs, 16, 23, 29, 89, 91
Fruit, 61; punch, 109
Funeral, 68
Fur, 90
Furniture, 17
Future, predictions of, 119

Gag, 19
Games, 23, 25, 26, 117
Gangsters, 19
Garage mechanic, 115
Garbage dump, 32
Gardener, 81, 83
Gardening, 62
Gas: pump, 120; tank, 115
Geese, 36
Geologist, 83
Geometric figure, 62, 96
Germ, 31
Ghost, 120, 122, 123, 124
Ghouls, 117, 119
Gingerbread Man, 51
Giraffes, 6
Gloves, 108
Gnome, 63
Gnus, 9
Goat, 13, 37
Golf, 108
Goose, 116
Gorilla, 10, 11, 71
Gossip, 24
Grapefruit, 47
Grapes, 63
Grass, 104; *see Lawns*
Great Wall of China, 98
Greetings, 78–80
Grindstone, 84
Gross, 92, 104
Gum, 45, 68, 72
Gun, 22, 66; powder, 103

Hair, 53; dryer, 9
Halloween, 64
Hammer, 72
Hands, of clock, 77
Hangman, 20
Hanky, 54
Hawaii, 25, 78
Hawk, 36
Haydn, 31

Hay: fever, 56, 104; stacks, 39
Helicopters, 44
Hen, 38; *see Chicken*
Herring, 42
Hiccups, 89
Hitchhiker, 116
Hockey player, 75
Hoe, 80
Holes, 58, 96
Holiday, 119
Hollywood, 123
Homing pigeon, 88
Honey, 72
Hop Scotch, 23
Horn, 26, 89
Horse, 12, 116; race, 107; wooden, 12
Hospital, 104, 114
Hot dog, 46, 118
House, 14, 63, 64, 104
Hyena, 13, 26

Ice, 71; berg, 55; cream, 83, 120; cube, 20, 32
Icing, 52
Illness, 52, 100–105
India, 48
Indians, 25, 52
Indigestion, 104
Insect, 15 73
Invisible Man, 29; and Woman, 119

Jail, 19
Jam, 47, 52
James, Jesse, 82
Jeans, 60
Jekyll, Dr., 23; and Mr. Hyde, 121
Jogger, 112
Jokes, 13, 24, 25, 31, 32, 34, 102, 124
Jolly Green Giant, 16, 50
Joseph, 61
Judges, 20, 112
Justice, 20

Kangaroo, 13, 45, 58
Karate school, 92
Khayyam, Omar, 77
King, 55; Arthur, 55; Cole, 48; Kong, 123
Kisses, 75
Knife sharpener, 83
Knight, 55, 123

Lady, 74
Lamb, 50
Laryngitis, 101
Last words, 69
Laughter, 30
Laundryman, 83
Lawns, 39, 104; *see Grass*

Lawn sprinkler, 9
Lawyer, 20, 81
Left and right, 71
Leg, wooden, 74
Leopard, 8
Letters, 65, 67, 74, 95, 96, 115
Letter-writers, 74
Library, 93
License plate, 113
Light, 67; bulb, 74
Lion, 13, 32, 58, 90, 102; tamer, 28
Lips, 57
Locomotive, 107
Lollipop, 53
Louis XIV, 55
Love, 73–77, 119
Luck, 74, 105
Lumberjacks, 68, 85
Lunch, 77

MacDonald, Old, 101
Machine gun, 22
Magazines, 62, 119
Magician, 117
Mail, 74, 90, 123; box, 58
Manners, 55
March, 64, 84
Marine scientist, 89
Mark Antony, 77
Marriage, 123
Martian, 120; band, 121
Matches, 25, 69, 109, 112
Mathematician, 52
May, 64
Meal, 44, 46, 50, 52
Meat loaf, 50
Medicine, 100, 103, 121
Mercedes Benz, 113
Mermaids, 77
Mickey Mouse, 105
Microwave, 41
Midgets, 79
Milk, 29, 63, 86; shake, 50
Milky Way, 36
Mind, making up, 72
Minister, 84
Mink, 43
Minnelli, Liza, 74
Mirror, 17, 24
Mittens, 90
Moat, 42
Monarchy, 55
Money, 37, 96
Monkeys, 11, 12: see Ape, Gorilla, King Kong
Monsters, 117–124
Moon, 36; beam, 62
Moose, 12
Morse code, 87
Moth, 15, 54
Motorist, 115
Mountains, 34, 53, 106

Mouse, 23, 54, 66, 105, 114
Moustache, 55
Movie stars, 115
Mummies, 124
Mumps, 100
Mushrooms, 63
Music, 26, 27, 30, 31, 33
Musical, 49
Musician, 33

Nail, 72; biting, 103
NBC, 95
New Delhi, 48
New Yorker, 102
Night watchman, 85
Noah, 25
Noise, 70
Nurse, 14
Nuts, 50, 53, 73

Occupations, 81–85
Ocean, 41, 43, 45
Octopus, 36, 43
Odds, 56
Officer, army, 54
Old: age, 99; King Cole, 48; MacDonald, 101
Opera, 31
Operations, 100
Orthodontist, 122
Oscar, 115
Otter, 13, 80
Outlaws, 19
Oven, 41
Overeating, 52
Owls, 40, 42
Oyster, 42

Pajama factory, 85
Pancakes, 69
Pants, 17, 20
Paper, 104
Paragraph, 95
Parents, 66
Parrot, 13, 35, 87, 88
Peanut, 71; butter, 8
Peanuts, 31
Pelican, 71
Pen, 94, 95
Pence, 96
Pencil, 53
Pets, 86–91
Phonograph: needle, 73; record, 71, 73
Pianist, 31
Piano tuner, 110
Pickle, 19, 25, 49, 57, 59, 65, 71, 74, 116; factory, 83
Pickpocket, 110
Picnic, 65
Picture, 22, 60
Pies, 52·
Pigs, 13, 37, 59
Pillow, 70

Pills, sleeping, 104
Pilot, 19, 84
Pitchers, 110
Pitchfork, 72
Pizza, 5, 51
Plants, 65
Plasma, 120
Plumber, 81
Poetry, 94
Poinsettia, 90
Pointer, 90
Poison ivy, 105
Police, 20
Pony, 104
Porcupine, 10
Portugal, 36
Postage stamp, 73
Post office, 70
Potato chips, 109
Potatoes, 20, 39
Pretzel, 50
Prince, 26; of Wales, 62
Principal, 92
Prisoners, 19
Professor, 92; absent-minded, 73
Protoplasm, 53
Prune, 77, 113
Psychiatrist, 26, 101
Pupil, 92
Puss, 86
Puzzle, 28

Rabbits, 9, 39, 115; electric, 80
Raccoon, 10
Races, 107, 113, 117; horse, 107
Rain, 70, 90, 102; drop, 55
Rainy season, 99
Rake, 80
Rally, 121
Ram, 36
Range, 66
Razor, 19
Real estate agents, 79
Record, 73
Records, world, 59-62
Referees, 112
Refrigerator, 66
Reindeer, 12
Relatives, 65, 122
Rest, 56
Restaurant: Chinese, 46; seafood, 44
Revolving door, 60, 65
Rhinoceros, 116
Rhythm, 33
Right and left, 71
Ring around the collar, 15
Riot, 70
Road, 47
Robbers, 19
Robin, 40

127

Robots, 50
Rock: concerts, 83; stars, 115
Rodent, 22
Roll, 31, 47
Roller skates, 115
Rolls-Royce, 115
Romans, 54, 107
Room, 63
Rooster, 6, 38, 40
Root beer, 69
Rope, 63
Roses, 73
Rubber band, 100
Rug, 103
Ruler, 58, 61
Running, 112

Safety, 123
Sailors, 41, 62, 78, 101
Salad, 49
Sandwiches, 48
Santa Claus, 65
Sap sucker, 10
Sardines, 42
Scarecrows, 79
Scarf, 18
School, 72, 92–99, 118
Scientist, marine, 89
Scissors, 63, 91
Screen, 63
Sea, 41, 45, 78; food restaurant, 44
Setter, 90
Shampoo, 53
Shark, 33, 87, 120
Sharpshooter, 35, 46
Sheep, 10
Sheets, 70
Shepherds, 83
Shillings, 96
Ship, 42; builder, 44
Shirt, 15; collars, 107
Shoes, 16
Shower, 104
Ski jump, 109
Skillet, 47
Skunks, 7, 10
Sky diving, 19
Sledding, 107
Sleeping pills, 104
Sleighing, 107
Smile, 55
Smoking, 67
Snacks, 50
Snacktime, 29
Snake, 9, 75, 111
Sneakers, 16, 112
Sneeze, 104
Snow, 107; ball, 26
Soap, 20, 48, 66
Soccer, 106
Socks, 17, 18
Soda, 29, 111

Soft drink, 69
Soldiers, 70, 79, 84
Song, 33, 72
Sorcerer, 117
Sorrow, 95
Soup, 48
Spaghetti, 8
Speech, 95
Spelling, 72
Spies, 52
Sponge, 49
Sports, 106-112
Spy, 21
Squid, 43
Squirrels, 73
Stairs, 66
Stampede, 70
Stamps, 73, 98
State, 99
Steam, 63
Stockings, 18, 63
Stove, 66
Strawberries, 52
Stream, 41
Stretcher, 100
Strike, 108, 110
Stupidity, 58
Sturgeon, 100
Suit, bathing, 81
Suits, 14, 15
Sun, 32, 46, 55, 105; tan, 47
Surfers, 78
Surgeon, 100
Survivors, 68
Suspense, 58
Swimmers, 120
Sword, 94; ballpoint, 54

Tadpoles, 91
Tailor, 17, 85, 91
Talkers, slowest, 60
Tarzan, 65, 69
Tea, 25
Teacher, 92
Teeth, 103
Telephones, 15, 54
Television, 23, 63
Tennis, 106
Termites, 50
Tests, 95, 96
Thieves, 19–22
Throat, sore, 121
Tide, 17, 107
Ties, 17, 107
Tiger, 46
Timbuktu, 99
Time, 55, 56, 94, 113, 114
Tire, 72
Tissue, 104
Toads, 88, 91, 113
Toasters, 58
Toilet, 108
Tomahawk, 36

Tomatoes, 49
Tonsils, 76
Tooth, 102; ache, 102; brush, 103; paste, 77, 103; pick, 72
Tow truck, 113
Toys, 26
Traffic, 41; light, 116; violation, 111
Train, 32, 68, 107, 114
Tramp, 32
Trapeze flyer, 28
Tree, 29, 36, 93
Troll, 63
Trousers, 17
Tuba, 31
Turkey, 33
Turtle, 13, 15
Tuxedo, 100

Umbrella, 55, 99
Umpire, 110, 111
U.N., 90
Unions, 110

Valentine's Day, 73
Vampires, 117, 118, 120, 122
Vanishing cream, 119
Vegetable, 20, 35
Ventriloquist, 84
Verse, blank, 94
Veterinarian, 112
Viking, 76
Violinist, 33
Vitamin, 103

Waitress, 120
Washington, George, 99
Watches, 20, 58, 67, 100
Watchmaker, 100
Water, 41, 104
Wave, 45
Weasel, 80
Weather, 74, 90, 108; forecaster, 85
Wednesday, 116
Weeds, 65
Werewolf, 118
Whales, 45, 62, 89
Window panes, 104
Witch, 117, 120, 121
Wolf, 38
Woodchopper, 36
Woodpecker, 58, 87
World records, 59–62
Worm, 10, 71
Wrestling, 112
Wrinkles, 103

Yard sale, 58
Yarn, 90

Zebra, 5
Zombie, 117, 119
Zoo, 46

128